WINDOWS
ON·THE·WORLD

ANIMALS
AND·WHERE·THEY·LIVE

By John Feltwell, Ph.D.

Publishers • GROSSET & DUNLAP • New York
A member of The Putnam Publishing Group

Contributing illustrators
John Rignall, Phil Weare, Ian Jackson,
Bob Bampton, Alan Male, Helen Senior,
Dee Morgan and Giuliano Fornari

Phototypeset by Southern Positives and Negatives (SPAN)
Reproduced in Singapore by Colourscan
Printed in Spain by Artes Graficas, Toledo S.A.
D. L. TO:1782 -1987

CONTENTS

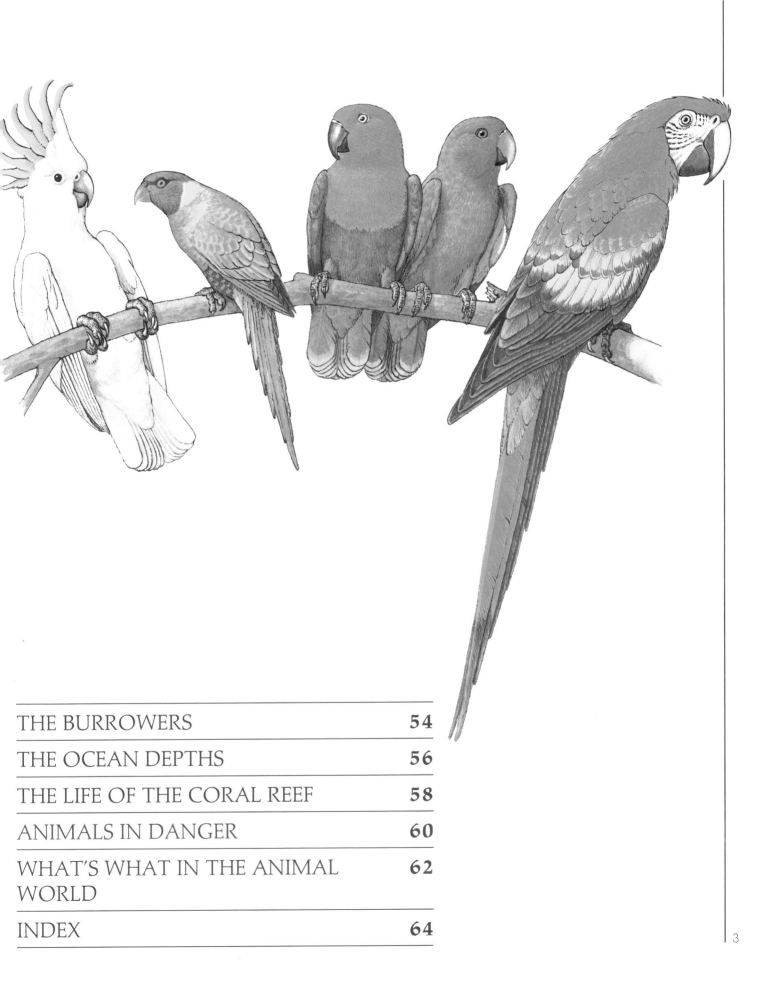

SPECIAL ANIMALS, SPECIAL PLACES

Just as we have our own special place to live, so animals have theirs. Animals live everywhere on Earth – on the land and in the sea, in every kind of terrain and in different types of climate. Most animals have lived in the same part of the world for thousands of years. As a result, they have developed a way of life that helps them fit into a particular place and climate. Each animal's own special living place is called its *habitat* or *environment*.

Because habitats are so different from each other, only certain animals can live in each one. Some fish, for example, need to live in fresh water. If they were put into the sea they would die. But a saltwater fish, such as a mackerel, could not survive if it were put into fresh water. For the same reason, penguins would die if moved to the desert, and scorpions would perish on the polar ice cap. It is true that you can go to a European or American safari park and see lions and other animals living quite happily, far from their original home on the African savannah. But many animals can be kept alive outside their natural habitats only if they are in zoos or aquariums. And while it is interesting to watch animals in captivity, to find out about how they really live we need to look at them in their natural surroundings.

Where animals live

By watching animals in their own habitats we can see how they find food, make their homes and bring up their young. We can also observe them as part of a whole community of different animals. Throughout the world, communities of animals live in widely differing habitats, ranging from burning deserts to the frozen wastes of the polar regions. By looking at each of the major environments around the world, we can find out more about how animals live.

A zoo in grand surroundings

Seeing different types of animals grouped together in the grand setting of a stately home makes you realize how very different our habitats are from those of animals. Can you imagine how you and your friends would look sitting in a rabbit warren or perched on top of a tree? In fact, all the animals in the picture can survive away from their natural habitats, provided they have food, warmth and shelter.

4

Snake

Owl

Spiny dormouse

Cat

Red squirrel

Bush baby

Alligator

Canary

Parakeet

Tortoise

Gerbil

Toad

Pigeon

Llama

Monkey

Kangaroo

Kestrel

Goat

Cheetah

Lion

Parrot

Raccoon

Otter

Guinea pig

Dog

Red fox

Lizard

Duck

Skunk

Weasel

Rabbit

Turtle

PICTURE MAP

The remarkable ability of animals to adapt to their surroundings has enabled them to colonize the wide variety of habitats that exist on Earth. Similar types of habitats are found in different places around the world and similar types of animals often live in them. The same kinds of animals live in the forests and tundra of North America and the U.S.S.R. Likewise, the same types of animals

graze on the grasslands of South America, Africa and Australia. The biggest habitat on Earth is the sea, which provides a home for some of the largest as well as the smallest creatures in the world. Wherever animals live, they have to compete for food and shelter. Nature maintains a fine balance so that different types of animals are able to live together in the same habitat.

Coniferous forest
A band of dense evergreen forest stretches across the top of Europe, Asia and North America. Forest animals have to be able to cope with long, hard winters. *See pages 20–21 for more on forests.*

Marshlands
Half land and half water, marshes are usually found near estuaries, lakes and rivers. They provide a home for a wide variety of wildlife, particularly birds. *See pages 34–35 for more on marshlands.*

Islands
All islands are different, and many of them provide a home for strange and totally unique plants and animals that are not found anywhere else in the world. *See pages 24–25 to find out about animals that live on islands.*

Oceans
The oceans cover about three-quarters of the Earth's surface. There are warm seas near the equator and frozen seas near the poles. *See pages 56–57 for more on oceans.*

Jungles
Jungles, or rain forests, grow near the equator, where it is hot and rains nearly every day. More types of plants and animals live there than anywhere else. *See pages 44–47 for more on jungles.*

Homes around the world
On this picture map you can see where the different types of habitats are all around the world. You can also see some of the animals that live in each area.

Arctic Ocean

North America

Rocky Mountains

Atlantic Ocean

Amazon jungle

South America

Antarctica

Polar regions
Amazingly, some animals and plants manage to thrive in the frozen wastes and seas of the Arctic and Antarctica. *See pages 8–11 for more on life in the polar regions.*

Shrublands
Sun-parched countryside, dotted with tough shrubs and aromatic herbs, is common around the Mediterranean. *See pages 26–29 for more on shrublands.*

Deciduous forests
Deciduous forests are found mostly in Europe and North America, where the climate is mild and damp. *See pages 22–23 to find out more about the life in a deciduous tree.*

Mountains
A wide range of habitats, ranging from lush forest on the lower slopes to bleak tundra higher up, can be found on a mountain. *See pages 14–17 to find out more about mountains.*

U.S.S.R.

Europe

Mediterranean Sea

Africa

Himalayas

Asia

Pacific Ocean

Equator

Savannah

Australia

Deserts
Deserts are the driest places on Earth. It rarely rains, but many plants and animals have adapted to life in these harsh conditions. *See pages 50–53 for more on deserts.*

Grasslands
The great grasslands of the world stretch for thousands of miles. These dry, grassy plains provide food for huge herds of grazing animals. *See pages 38–41 for more on grasslands.*

Coral reefs
A coral reef is an exotic underwater kingdom, teeming with animals and plants. Reefs are found in shallow, sunlit, tropical waters. *See pages 58–59 for more on coral reefs.*

A WORLD OF ICE

The polar regions are a hostile world of ice and snow. The winters can last for up to nine months, with sub-zero temperatures, raging blizzards and total darkness for much of the time. During the brief summer months there is daylight for nearly 24 hours a day. The temperature rises above freezing and some of the ice melts. It seems as if nothing could live in these frozen wastes, yet, astonishingly, there are many plants and animals that survive and even flourish there.

The Arctic Ocean stretches across the North Pole. The ocean is covered with ice for most of the year, yet fish, seals and whales live there in vast numbers, feeding on the rich supply of *algae*, tiny plants that live in it. The ocean is surrounded by frozen land called tundra. Tough bushes and plants grow on the tundra, and in the spring and summer it comes alive with insects, birds and small animals, such as lemmings and hares.

Conditions are even harder on Antarctica, the frozen continent around the South Pole. Little survives on Antarctica itself, but the seas around it are swarming with life. Here and on the next two pages we take a closer look at life in a world of ice.

Polar bear
The polar bear is an excellent swimmer and its thick fur keeps it warm in the water as well as on land. It spends most of its time roaming the sea ice in search of seals to eat.

Arctic terns
Like many other birds, the Arctic tern is a summer visitor to the Arctic and it nests along the coasts. In the autumn it migrates all the way to Antarctica, where summer is coming.

Walruses
Walruses usually live in herds. They move northward with the ice pack as it melts in spring and swim south ahead of the freezing sea in autumn, feeding on shellfish from the seabed.

Arctic terns

Beluga

Polar bear

Oldsquaw ducks

Blackfish

Cod

The great thaw
When spring arrives in the Arctic, the ice begins to thaw. Flowers come into bloom on the tundra and there is a sudden burst of activity among the animals. As food supplies become more plentiful, birds start nesting on the high cliffs overlooking the ice and animals rear their young.

Narwhal
The male narwhal whale has a strange, long, twisted tusk that looks rather like a unicorn's horn. No one knows what it is used for, but males have been seen sparring with them.

Cod and blackfish
In spring, huge shoals of cod and blackfish swim into the Arctic Ocean to feed on the plankton and to spawn. They provide valuable food for the seals and seabirds.

Skuas and jaegers
Both of these birds are predators. Skuas like to steal other birds' food and will eat any dead birds or animals (carrion) they find. Jaegers are long-tailed skuas and eat mainly lemmings.

Puffins and murres
Huge colonies of puffins and murres nest on steep cliffs above the ice. Puffins lay their eggs in shallow burrows in soft clifftop soil. Murres nest on narrow ledges. Their eggs are pear-shaped, so do not roll.

Puffins

Skuas

Jaegers

Murres

Hooded seals

Harp seals

Bearded seal

Hooded seals
Seals spend most of their lives in the sea, but come onto the ice to mate and breed. These males have large noses, which they inflate like balloons when they are courting.

Ringed seal
This seal also lives mainly in the sea, but it can stay underwater for only 20 minutes at a time. It chews breathing holes in the ice, so that it can come up for air.

Ivory gulls
Ivory gulls are the only seabirds that are totally white in color. This helps to protect them from predators, because the gulls are difficult to see against the snow.

Bear families
Female polar bears give birth to their cubs in the safety of a snow den, deep inside a snow bank. The mother goes without food for up to six months while she looks after her cubs.

SURVIVING THE COLD

The animals and birds that live near the poles have adapted in unique ways to cope with life in icy conditions. Furry animals such as polar bears and foxes have a thick outer coat of long, shaggy hair and a soft, fleecy layer of fur closer to their skin, so they are doubly protected against the cold. Whales, polar bears and seals have thick layers of fat called blubber under their skin, and birds that spend the winter in the polar regions have thick plumage and fluff out their feathers to keep themselves warm. Some insects hibernate in the winter, and have a special chemical in their blood which acts like anti-freeze and stops their blood from freezing.

The animals that live on land or ice have to be able to walk across the snow easily. Polar bears have big, wide feet that act like snowshoes, and birds such as ptarmigans and grouse have feathers on the soles of their feet.

As well as coping with the cold, animals have to time very carefully when they mate and give birth. Most animals breed during the brief summer months when it is warmer and food is plentiful.

Breeding on the ice
Penguins are the only birds that are able to breed in the freezing conditions on Antarctica. Most of them breed in the spring in huge rookeries inland from the sea, but the emperor penguins, shown here, breed on the ice-covered sea in the depths of winter.

The largest penguins
The emperor penguins are the largest of all penguins. They can be 4 feet (1.2m) tall. Like all penguins, they are admirably adapted to life in the water. Their short wings act as paddles, their webbed feet help them to steer, and their bodies are streamlined in shape.

Speedy swimmers
Penguins cannot fly and they look clumsy on land. They waddle along or slither on their bellies. They are more at home underwater, where they can swim at up to 25 miles per hour (40kph). To get back on the ice, they shoot out of the water and land upright on their feet.

Winter eggs
Emperors do not breed at the same time as other penguins, but in the middle of winter, when the temperature is well below freezing. The male and female penguins have very different roles. The female lays a single egg, and immediately dives into the sea and swims away.

Incubating the egg

The male penguin balances the egg on his feet and covers it with part of his body, a sort of pouch, to keep it warm. For 64 days, in pitch darkness and through blizzards, the penguin stands there, incubating the egg.

The chick hatches

During that time, the penguin does not eat and gets much thinner. When the ice breaks up in the spring, the female returns, just as the chick hatches. The male is free to go and find food, then both parents care for the chick.

Changing color

Many of the animals and birds that live in the Arctic change the color of their feathers or fur with the changing seasons, so that they are well camouflaged all the year round. They do this by molting. Predators, such as Arctic foxes, have coats that change from brown in the summer to white in the winter. So do the creatures they prey on, such as hares and ptarmigans. If they all stayed brown in winter, they would easily be seen against the white snow.

Arctic fox

Arctic hare

Ptarmigan

Winter underground

In the Arctic winter, while many animals sleep, life carries on beneath the snow. Lemmings live in a maze of burrows and runs below the surface of the tundra, and the layers of snow act like a quilt, helping to keep them warm. The lemmings feed on roots and underground shoots and carry on breeding all winter. They do not emerge from the burrows until the snow melts in late spring and food is more plentiful above the ground.

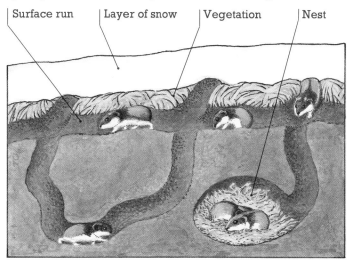

Surface run | Layer of snow | Vegetation | Nest

THE LARGEST ANIMALS

The largest animals ever to roam the Earth were the dinosaurs, which died out 65 million years ago. The largest of them may have been as long as 74 feet (22.5m) and weighed up to 90 tons.

Nowadays the African elephant is the largest animal living on land, but in both size and weight it is dwarfed by the largest animal of all: the blue whale. This marine giant is both longer and heavier than the biggest dinosaur that ever lived. For the blue whale it is actually an advantage to be big. Its great size helps it to keep warm in cold water.

How large an animal is depends on where it lives and what it eats. The elephant is probably big partly because it needs a big stomach to digest all the tough plants it eats. Its size also helps to protect it, as few predators would dare to attack it.

Large animals used to have few enemies, but now they are at the mercy of the most dangerous predators of all, humans, and many of them are being hunted to the point of extinction.

The giants of the animal world
Here some of the biggest animals are grouped together to show how big they are in relation to each other. As you can see, those that live on land are dwarfed by those that live in the sea.

The biggest animal
The blue whale is the biggest mammal in the world. It is over 100 feet (30m) long and can weigh up to 190 tons. Incredibly for its size, the blue whale has no teeth and lives entirely on a diet of tiny shrimplike creatures called krill.

The largest fish
The rare plankton-eating whale shark is about 56 feet (17m) long and weighs 37 tons. This makes it the biggest fish in the world.

Tallest living mammal
The average height of the Masai giraffe of East Africa is 17 feet, 4½ inches (5.3m), making it taller than any other animal. With its long neck it feeds from the tops of acacia trees and thorny bushes on the plains where it lives.

The largest on land
The African elephant stands about 10½ feet (3.2m) tall at the shoulder and weighs over 5 tons. It once roamed over most of Africa, but its numbers have now declined and it is confined mainly to wildlife parks and game reserves.

The biggest bird
At 8 feet (2.4m) tall, the African ostrich is the largest bird in the world. It is also the fastest-running bird, as it can run at speeds of up to 30 miles per hour (48kph), but it cannot fly. Other giant flightless birds are the emu, the rhea and the cassowary.

Elephant

Man

Ostrich

Giraffe

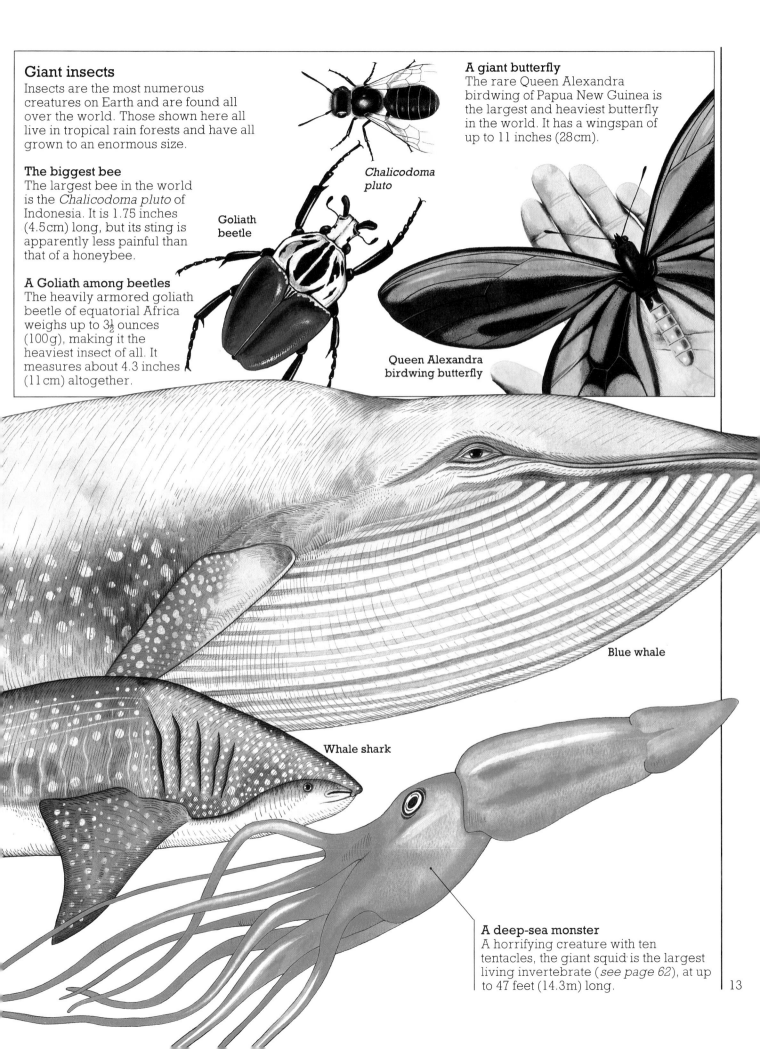

Giant insects

Insects are the most numerous creatures on Earth and are found all over the world. Those shown here all live in tropical rain forests and have all grown to an enormous size.

The biggest bee

The largest bee in the world is the *Chalicodoma pluto* of Indonesia. It is 1.75 inches (4.5cm) long, but its sting is apparently less painful than that of a honeybee.

A Goliath among beetles

The heavily armored goliath beetle of equatorial Africa weighs up to 3½ ounces (100g), making it the heaviest insect of all. It measures about 4.3 inches (11cm) altogether.

Chalicodoma pluto

Goliath beetle

A giant butterfly

The rare Queen Alexandra birdwing of Papua New Guinea is the largest and heaviest butterfly in the world. It has a wingspan of up to 11 inches (28cm).

Queen Alexandra birdwing butterfly

Blue whale

Whale shark

A deep-sea monster

A horrifying creature with ten tentacles, the giant squid is the largest living invertebrate (*see page 62*), at up to 47 feet (14.3m) long.

LIFE IN THE MOUNTAINS

On every mountain, within the short distance from its base to its peak, there is a wide variety of different habitats, ranging from dense forest to bare, rocky ground. This is because weather conditions change all the way up a mountain. The lower slopes often have a lot of mist or rain, but as you climb higher, the air becomes cooler and drier. This affects the types of trees and plants that grow at each level, and from a distance quite distinct bands of vegetation can be seen merging into each other all the way up the mountain.

As you climb a mountain, you move first through tropical or deciduous forest, depending on which part of the world you are in, then into coniferous forest. Next you come to the "tree line," where the trees end. No trees can grow above this height, which varies depending on the weather conditions and where the mountain is. Above the tree line are grassy meadows, then rocky ground and finally, on high mountains, a snow-covered peak. Different animals live in each band of vegetation.

Life at different levels
Here you can see how the plant and animal life changes at different levels on an imaginary mountain in the Himalayas. The highest mountains in the world, the Himalaya range is 1,500 miles (2,400km) long and 20,000 feet (6,000m) high on average.

Lammergeier

Wild yak

Markhor goats

Apollo butterfly

Lesser panda

Snowcocks

Black bear

Tiger

Greylag geese

Snow leopard

Snow and rocks
It is very cold at the top of a high mountain and no plants can grow there. The Himalayas are so high that their peaks are covered with snow and ice all year round. The snow leopard occasionally ventures up high and sharp-eyed birds of prey soar above the slopes.

Wolf

Argali

Alpine tundra
The tundra zone is similar in appearance to the Arctic tundra (*see page 10*). The rocky ground is dotted with icy pools in winter and sprinkled with flowers in spring. Grazing animals like the wild yak and the argali, Asia's largest mountain sheep, graze there in the summer.

Himalayan monal

Wild asses

Alpine meadow
Above the tree line are lush, grassy meadows. It is still very cold here and plants have to be tough to survive the harsh conditions. They have long roots and grow close to the ground. Wild asses and mountain goats like the markhor graze on the meadows in the summer.

Bhutan glory

Tahr

Pikas

Coniferous forests
Conifers, such as the pine and fir, flourish in the cold, dry mountain air. Their resin protects them from hungry insects, but their cones provide seeds for birds to eat. The lesser panda, an agile tree climber, lives in these forests, as does the tahr, a type of mountain goat.

Serows (goat antelopes)

Langur

Deciduous forests
The deciduous forests of the foothills provide food and shelter for a wide variety of animals. Langur monkeys eat the fruit and leaves of the trees and move higher up the mountain during the summer. Bears and tigers roam the forested slopes at the base of the mountain.

15

LIFE AT THE TOP

The higher you go up a mountain, the colder the air becomes, dropping by 3.6°F (2°C) every 1,000 feet (300m) you climb. It also becomes thinner and contains less oxygen. Mountain animals have thick, warm fur and strong lungs to help them cope with the cold, the wind and snow, and the thin air. They are also sure-footed, so that they don't lose their grip on steep, rocky slopes. Many animals move up the mountain to the lush alpine pastures in the summer, once the snow has melted, but return to the lower slopes or even the valleys in winter. Other animals hibernate to avoid the winter cold.

On the roof of the world
Because of the way they have adapted to mountain life, unrelated animals from different mountain areas look alike. Similar goats and sheep, small plant-eaters and predators live in mountain ranges all around the world.

Grazers
Many large grazing animals find food and refuge on the lush alpine pastures of mountains in the summer. Related to domestic goats, sheep and cattle, they include the bighorn sheep and mountain goats of North America and the Barbary sheep of North Africa. They have thick, woolly coats and long, curly horns, and are remarkably agile, bounding up and down the mountain from one steep, rocky ledge to another without slipping.

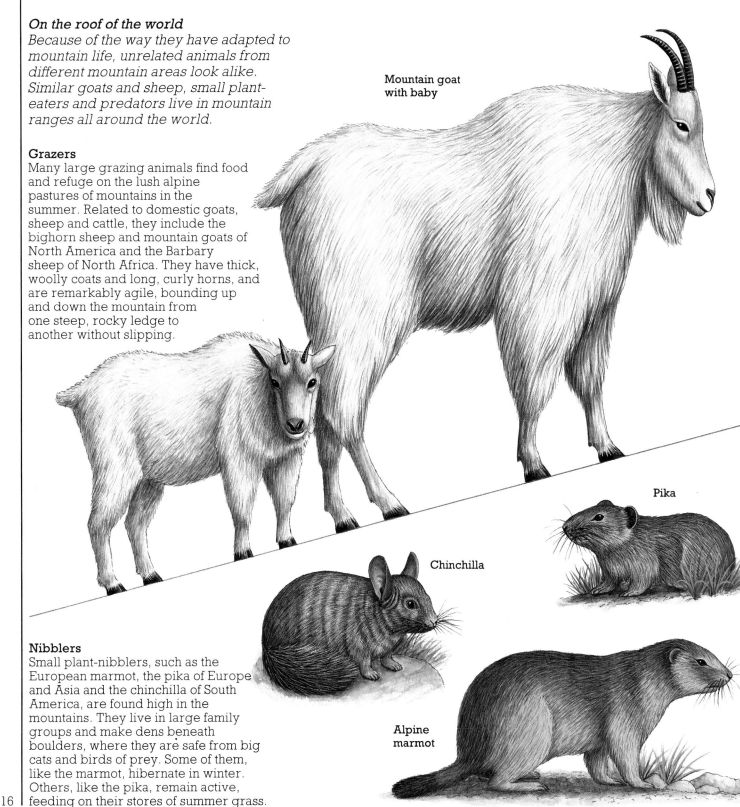

Mountain goat with baby

Pika

Chinchilla

Alpine marmot

Nibblers
Small plant-nibblers, such as the European marmot, the pika of Europe and Asia and the chinchilla of South America, are found high in the mountains. They live in large family groups and make dens beneath boulders, where they are safe from big cats and birds of prey. Some of them, like the marmot, hibernate in winter. Others, like the pika, remain active, feeding on their stores of summer grass.

Barbary sheep

Bighorn sheep

Lynx

Cougar

Predators

Even steep slopes cannot keep plant-eaters safe from carnivores. Big cats prey on the grazers and nibblers in most mountains. The lynx of Europe and America, the American puma and the Asian snow leopard spend summer high above the tree line. Their dappled coats help to camouflage them among rocks and trees. The snow leopard has broad, furry foot pads like snowshoes.

Snow leopard

LIFE ON THE WING

The most accomplished flyers of the animal world are birds. They are not the only animals that can fly – insects and bats can,too – but birds can fly farther and faster than any other animal. They have perfected the art of flying. They can soar in the air for hours, swoop at breakneck speeds, land on water and perform astonishing aerobatics. Some of them can also catch their food, mate and feed their young on the wing.

Birds are admirably suited to flying. They have powerful wings, streamlined bodies and lots of energy. Most important of all, however, they are equipped with feathers. Not only are these waterproof and warm, they also act as aerofoils on birds' wings, enabling birds to take off and maneuver in the air. It is feathers that give the birds their unique flying ability.

The masters of the air
Here are some of the record-holders among birds: those that fly the farthest, the fastest and the highest. Each of them is uniquely adapted to the life it leads.

The longest wingspan
With a wingspan of about 10 feet (3m), the wandering albatross has the longest wingspan of any bird. Its long, thin wings are the same shape as a glider's, and rather like a glider, it can soar effortlessly over the ocean for hours once it has gained height.

An aerial acrobat
A master of hovering and maneuvering, the hummingbird can fly backward as well as forward and do all sorts of aerobatics. It can tilt its wings in any direction, which means that it can hover perfectly still in front of a flower while it feeds on the nectar inside it. It flaps its wings so fast – 50 to 80 times a second – that they make the characteristic humming sound which gives the bird its name.

A mighty bird
The Andean condor is the heaviest bird of prey in the world, weighing up to 24 pounds (11 kg). Its huge wings enable it to soar the skies for hours, scarcely needing to flap its wings.

The great travellers
The Arctic tern is the greatest long-distance flyer among birds. It flies from the Arctic to Antarctica and back every year – a distance of about 25,000 miles (40,200 km). The sooty tern can spend 3 to 4 years in the air at a stretch.

Arctic tern

Sooty tern

High flyers
In 1967 a flock of whooper swans was spotted by the pilot of an airplane as they were flying at a height of about 26,900 feet (8,200 m) – the greatest flying height for birds ever recorded.

The fastest seabird
The fastest flying seabird known is the magnificent frigate bird. Its wings can be up to 8 feet (2.4 m) long and enable it to fly at a top speed of 95.6 miles per hour (154 kph).

Flying by sonar
Bats are the only true flying mammals and they hunt at night for insects – or fruit, if they are fruit bats. Although not blind, they use a kind of sonar system to find their way and to track down prey. They make high-pitched sounds, then pick up the returning echoes, using their large, sensitive ears as receptors. In this way they can locate any object around them. Contrary to belief, most bats are clean, harmless, sociable and highly intelligent.

Long-eared bats have especially big ears and good hearing. They are able to hover while searching for food.

19

DEEP IN THE FOREST

Across the northern tips of Europe, Asia and North America lies a thick band of dense evergreen forest. Tall conifers such as pine, fir and spruce grow close together and their thickly leaved branches cut out so much light that few plants can grow beneath them. It is only in clearings or by rivers and lakes that other plants grow.

The winters are long and bitterly cold in the northern forests, and the ground is deep in snow for up to six months a year. The trees have to be tough to survive the icy cold. They have hard, waxy needles instead of leaves, and their branches slope downward, so that snow can slide off them easily.

The same types of animals live throughout the northern forests and they too have adapted to the hard conditions and seasonal changes. Many of them hibernate during the winter or migrate to warmer feeding grounds. The animals that remain active store up food during the warm summer months to keep them going through the winter. Many of them also have coats that turn white in the winter, to help camouflage them against the snow.

The forest appears to be a dark, quiet place where nothing much is happening, but in spring and summer it comes to life.

A quiet backwater
Deep in the pine forests of North America, animals gather near a river to feed, drink and make their nests and homes during the brief weeks of summer. Small birds and animals gather seeds from the trees and beavers are busily building a dam, while larger animals search for food to help see them through the winter.

Black bear
The black bear is very good at climbing trees. It spends every day looking for food: scooping honey from hives, collecting berries, searching for dead animals and even fishing.

Woodpeckers
Woodpeckers are admirably suited to forest life. They nest in holes in trees and feed on insects, extracting them from the bark of the tree with their long tongues.

Hairy woodpecker

Pileated woodpecker

Spruce grouse

Crossbill
Crossbills live high in the trees and eat pine seeds. Their "crossed" bills help them to extract the seeds from pinecones. They regurgitate them to feed to their young.

Nighttime creatures

The raccoon sleeps in trees during the day, but at night it looks for food along the riverbank. It eats almost anything it finds, but washes its food carefully first.

The fisher is a large weasellike animal. It lives mostly in trees and can move very fast, outrunning a squirrel. It preys on porcupines and other small animals.

An acute sense of hearing, good eyesight, a hooked bill and sharp talons make the long-eared owl a fierce predator of small animals. Its long "ears" are really only tufts of feathers.

Red squirrel
The red squirrel spends its life scurrying up and down trees, using its bushy tail to help it balance. It eats huge amounts of pine seeds, leaving piles of empty pinecones behind.

Moose
The moose is the largest deer in the world and an excellent swimmer. It spends its summers near lakes, streams and bogs, feeding on the water plants that grow there.

Beavers
Beavers build dams across forest streams, using trees they have felled with their teeth. In the pond they build a "lodge," a dome-shaped home of sticks with underwater entrances.

Wolverine
The wolverine is the largest of all weasels and is very fierce. It is extremely strong for its size and will attack almost anything. An adult can catch and kill a reindeer by itself.

Northern goshawk

Mourning-cloak butterfly

American redstart

Pine marten

Yellow-rumped warbler

Moose

Wolverine

Beaver

Eastern chipmunk

Snowshoe hare
The snowshoe hare is on the constant lookout for danger, with its large ears pricked. In summer its coat is dark brown, but as winter approaches, it turns snowy white.

Lynx
An agile predator with small pointed ears and a spotted coat, the lynx stalks prey such as rabbits, or small deer. It belongs to the cat family and is an agile climber.

Swallowtail
Butterflies like the swallowtail make the most of the brief summer months, drinking nectar and laying their eggs on wild flowers. They often settle near water.

Porcupine
The porcupine has strong claws which help it to climb trees in search of bark to eat. Porcupines defend themselves from predators by raising their sharp, barbed quills.

THE WORLD OF A TREE

A single tree provides food, shelter and a hunting ground for an astonishing variety of wildlife. Owls and squirrels sleep in holes in the trunk, birds nest in the branches, spiders hide in cracks in the bark, and hundreds of insects live among the leaves.

A tree and its inhabitants form a food chain. The tree makes its food from water and minerals in the soil, and from sunlight. Its leaves, flowers, fruit and even the wood itself are eaten by the insects, birds and small mammals that live in it. These creatures are eaten by bigger animals, which in turn eventually die and rot back into the soil. So a tree is rather like a miniature world of its own.

The life of a deciduous tree, such as the oak, follows a yearly cycle. There is frantic activity in the spring and summer, when birds are feasting on the insects that are feeding on the new leaves. This is followed by a calmer period in autumn and winter. The tree loses its leaves and the animals become less active, some migrating while others hibernate.

The tree in autumn
On a mild autumn day, the golden leaves of the oak are beginning to fall. Squirrels and woodpeckers are enjoying insects and ripe acorns, and birds fly in and out of the branches of the tree, while below, the litter of dead leaves is teeming with its own animal life.

Green oak tortrix moth
The oak tortrix moth spends the day resting on the underside of an oak leaf. Oak tortrix caterpillars feed on young oak leaves in spring and can make the tree look quite bare.

Oak apples and gall wasps
Oak apples are not apples; inside each one is the white larva of a gall wasp. The female lays an egg in an oak bud and the "apple" forms around the egg, protecting it while it develops.

Red admiral
The red admiral is a fast flyer and patrols a small territory of its own, chasing away intruding butterflies. It often rests and suns itself with outstretched wings.

Lesser spotted woodpecker
This bird prefers old oak trees. It works hard for hours, digging out insects from the bark. It is rarely seen, but can often be heard pecking at a rate of up to 15 times a second.

Tree creeper
This tiny brown bird runs up tree trunks, hunting for insects. Its curved bill is ideal for plucking them out of the bark, and its strong claws enable it to cling tightly to the tree trunk.

Stag beetles
The larvae of these beetles live in the leaf litter beneath the oak tree. Adult males often fight each other, using their huge mandibles in the same way that stags use their antlers.

Wood lice
Wood lice live in the moist leaf litter beneath the oak tree. They would dry out in sunshine, so they are active only at night, feeding on decaying leaves, bark and fungus.

Green woodpecker
Although it nests in a hole in the oak tree, this bird probes for insects in the grass, rather than in the bark of the tree. It rarely makes the typical tapping sound of a woodpecker.

Long-tailed tits

Jay

Tree creeper

Red admiral

Wood pigeons

Long-tailed tits
Long-tailed tits use their tails to help them balance on twigs in the leafy branches of the oak while they search for insects. Their nests are balls of moss, feathers and lichen.

Gray squirrel
The acrobatic gray squirrel scurries from tree to tree, collecting ripe acorns to eat or store for the winter. It makes a winter nest, called a drey, close to the tree trunk.

Jay
This noisy, colorful bird eats all kinds of food, even young birds. In the autumn it buries acorns in the ground, and in winter it returns to its hidden food stores to feed.

Nuthatch
The nuthatch walks down the tree trunk and eats the insects the tree creeper missed. It also eats acorns, wedging them in the bark and opening them with its ''hatchet'' beak.

Wood pigeons
Wood pigeons may build their nests – flat platforms of twigs – in oak trees. They eat mainly farm crops and raise their young in late summer when the year's harvest is ripening.

Wood ants
These large ants make huge nests with many tunnels from twigs and dead leaves. They prey on insects and often kill them by spraying them with formic acid.

Earwig
The earwig is a small, beetlelike creature with large pincers at the back end of its body. Earwigs like dark places to hide and are active at night, looking for food.

Ladybug
Not all ladybugs are black and red; some are yellow and black. They are useful to the oak tree, as they eat hundreds of aphids – the bugs that suck its sap – every day.

23

ISLAND CASTAWAYS

Some of the strangest animals in the world live on islands, where they have been cut off from mainland continents for millions of years. No two islands are the same and many of them, such as the Galapagos Islands, Madagascar, Mauritius and Australia, have unique plants and animals. Some animals, though similar to others elsewhere, have grown to enormous sizes, while others are tiny (*see pages 36–37*). Some creatures look as if they haven't changed for millions of years and others are unique and completely different from anything else anywhere in the world.

Island animals are unusual because thousands of years of isolation have caused them to evolve

Strange and unusual animals
Here a group of strange animals from different islands all around the world have been brought together. Each one is unique in its own way.

Galapagos tortoise

Proboscis monkey

Giant monitor lizard

Tuatara

Giant animals
Many island animals grow larger than their relatives elsewhere. The giant monitor lizard of Komodo in Indonesia is the largest lizard in the world, being up to 10 feet (3m) long. It is a fierce hunter.

The giant tortoises of the Galapagos Islands are truly enormous – up to 39 inches (1m) long. They are completely vegetarian and grow bigger as they grow older. They can live up to 50 years.

An unusual monkey
The odd-looking proboscis monkey is a very good swimmer and lives only on Borneo, in mangrove swamps. The male has an enormous, droopy nose that it inflates to make its loud call.

A prehistoric reptile
The tuatara of New Zealand is the only survivor of a group of reptiles that lived 140 million years ago. On top of its head it has an extra eye covered with skin. No one knows why.

differently from their relatives on the mainland. These different and sometimes strange-looking animals have become perfectly adapted to island life, where there is little competition for food and often no predators to fear. Their isolation has made them vulnerable to interference from outside, and many of them have become extinct since being "discovered" by humans (*see pages 60–61*).

Cassowary

Red kangaroo

Platypus

Koala bears

Wombat

An island of marsupials
In Australia and Tasmania there are many different kinds of marsupials. All of them rear their young in pouches. Koala bears live in trees and eat nothing but eucalyptus leaves. Kangaroos roam the grasslands. They can bound along at speeds of up to 30 miles per hour (48kph). The wombat is an energetic digger. It lives in woods and leaves its burrow only at night to go looking for food.

An odd animal
The duck-billed platypus of Australia is very strange. It is a mammal and lays eggs. It has webbed feet and can swim and dive like an otter. It has a bill like a duck's, and a hairy coat, typical of a mammal.

Fierce and flightless
The fierce-looking cassowary of New Guinea and Australia is one of the many flightless birds to evolve on islands. It uses the bony lump on its head to push its way through the rain forests where it lives.

DAY AND NIGHT IN THE SHRUBLAND

In southern Europe and around the Mediterranean, the main type of countryside is shrubland. The dry and sometimes hilly land is covered with heath and heavily scented herbs, and dotted with thorny shrubs, small evergreen oak trees and clumps of broom. The summers here are long, hot and very dry and the winters are mild and wet. Any plants that grow in this dry, sun-drenched landscape have to be drought-resistant. They have long roots and tough leathery leaves that conserve moisture and help them to last for months without rain. Most of the flowers bloom briefly in the spring and early summer, before the heat of the sun shrivels them.

Many different animals live in this type of shrubland and they have also adapted to the high summer temperatures and lack of rain. Lizards and insects thrive in the heat. Frogs, toads and snakes often bury themselves in dried-up riverbeds or hide under rocks to keep cool. Some butterflies rest during the hottest months of the year and become active only in the autumn. Others move to cooler areas where they can find more food.

Many animals rest during the day and come out to feed only as dusk falls and the temperature drops, so both by day and by night the shrubland is constantly alive with animals. On these two pages you can see the animals that come out during the day, and on the next two pages you can see how the scene changes at night.

Golden oriole
The male golden oriole has exotic yellow and black plumage, but the female looks like a green woodpecker. Fast flyers, they dart from tree to tree. They migrate in the winter.

Wood ants
Wood ants spray powerful formic acid in the face of an attacking predator. Large colonies of wood ants can continue for several decades and have up to 300,000 worker ants.

Green woodpecker

Red squirrel

Wood ants

Black-veined white butterfly

In the heat of the day
As the sun rises high in the sky, the air becomes hot, still and heavy with the aroma of wild herbs. Bees and wasps buzz around the sweetly scented herbs and shrubs, and there is the constant humming sound of millions of grasshoppers and cicadas that are concealed in the grass and shrubs. Occasionally a lizard which has been basking on a rock in the sun scuttles for shelter. It looks at first as if there is nothing much to see, but really an astonishing variety of creatures live in the tough conditions of this sun-parched landscape.

Green lizards
Basking on bare earth or rocks within easy reach of a hiding place, the green lizard is alert to both danger and any insects it can eat. Only the male has the superb blue throat.

Weasel
The weasel is active by both day and night and follows a regular hunting route. It hunts rodents and rabbits, and kills them by repeatedly biting the backs of their necks.

Wildcat
The ancestor of the domestic cat, the wildcat makes its den in a hollow log among rocks and trees. Seldom seen, it hunts birds and rodents by both day and night.

Great gray shrike
An aggressive bird, the great gray shrike is also called the "butcher bird." It catches insects and lizards, then impales them on thorny bushes which it uses as a "pantry."

Buzzard
The buzzard may often be seen soaring over the wooded or rocky areas where it breeds, on the lookout for small animals. As soon as it spots a victim, it swoops down on it.

Hoopoe
Named after its unusual call, "hoo-poo," this bird has an attractive plume on its head. It uses its long bill to probe the ground for insects and usually nests in a hollow tree.

Wildcat

Great gray shrike

Apollo butterfly

Rabbits

Marbled white butterfly

Stag beetle

Burnet moth

Scarce swallowtail
This butterfly flits from flower to flower in search of nectar. Its long "tails" look like antennae. This confuses attacking birds and gives the butterfly a chance to escape.

Rabbits
When grazing, rabbits have to be on a constant lookout for predators. They have no means of defense, but they can hear well and run fast. They live together in warrens.

Honeybees
Busily searching for nectar, worker honeybees visit thousands of flowers, herbs and trees during the summer. They take nectar back to their hive, where it is made into honey.

Argiope spider
The argiope spider spins its web over plants to ensnare butterflies and flies. The spider's bright coloring deters birds from eating it, as they think it might be poisonous.

Beech marten
A member of the weasel family, the beech marten is a stealthy nighttime forager and feeds on wild fruit and berries. Its bushy tail helps it to balance when it climbs trees.

Barn owl
Like a phantom, the white barn owl flaps its way silently through the night, hunting for small animals and roosting birds, which it swoops upon. Its call is an eerie shriek.

Roe deer
The timid roe deer emerges from woodland at dusk to browse at the edge of the trees. If it sees any sign of danger, it gives a sharp, doglike bark as a warning signal to others.

Serotine bats
Using sonar to find their prey, these large bats catch moths and beetles in their wings. Some moths are able to move out of the line of attack, as they can pick up the bats' soundwaves.

Roe
deer

Beech
marten

Spurge hawk moth
The caterpillars of this moth feed on poisonous plants called spurges. The bright colors of both caterpillar and moth warn birds and lizards that they are poisonous.

Stick insect
The stick insect is hard to see, as it blends in so well with grass stems and twigs. Its body, legs and antennae are all long and thin, which help to make it look like part of a plant.

Red fox
The fox is secretive and intelligent. It hunts by night, preying on birds and small mammals. The vixen teaches her cubs to hunt by taking them on nightly expeditions.

Smooth snake
At night, smooth snakes come out of their daytime resting places under stones or in crevices to feed on lizards and other small animals. They can live for up to 20 years.

Wild boar

Foraging for insects and roots, wild boars dig up the ground at twilight. They lead a solitary life, but a sow with a litter of piglets will attack fiercely if threatened.

Little owl

This small, flat-headed owl flies low over the shrubland at night and hunts at dusk. It bobs up and down when curious about something. It nests in hollow trees.

A twilight world

As dusk falls, the daytime animals retire to rest and the shrubland is taken over by a completely different group of animals. Crickets take up the constant droning of the daytime grasshoppers and cicadas and there is the occasional hoot of an owl. Fireflies flash in the dark, sending messages to each other, and nocturnal caterpillars emerge to feed safely on plants, unseen by the sleeping birds. Bats flit through the sky as they leave their roosts to hunt for insects until dawn.

Many small mammals and some reptiles are active at night, foraging for their food in the undergrowth. Sharp-eyed predators, such as foxes and the silent-flying owls, leave their daytime resting places as dusk falls to hunt these nighttime creatures. Here you can see how the animals use the cover of darkness for their nocturnal activities.

Scops owl

Wild boars

Giant peacock moth

Marsh frog

Giant peacock moth

This moth has large eye markings in the center of both its upper and under wings. Their similarity to the markings on a peacock's tail gives the moth its name.

Badger

Badgers live together in groups. Active at night, they go on walks, leaving dung to mark their territory. They eat mostly earthworms in summer and roots in winter.

European tree frogs

These little frogs croak loudly at night. They are more likely to be found on twigs than in water. Their shape and color help to camouflage them among the trees and shrubs.

Scorpion

A nocturnal prowler, the scorpion searches for small insects, such as earwigs and caterpillars. It stuns its prey with its stinging tail, which it arches forward over its back.

COUNTRY TO CITY

At first sight the hustle and bustle of a big city seems an unlikely place to find a wealth of wildlife. But animals have an amazing ability to adapt, changing their living and feeding habits to survive in a new environment. Blackbirds, sparrows and mice are well-known city residents, but there are many unexpected visitors too. The animals found in cities range from raccoons and coyotes in North America, to foxes and squirrels in Europe and kangaroos in Australia.

Many animals move from the countryside to the city because their natural habitat is under threat. Trees are pulled down and undergrowth cleared to make room for new roads and houses. The city offers them shelter, food and warmth. The large number of buildings in the city make it warmer than the countryside, and garbage dumps provide well-stocked pantries for all kinds of greedy scavengers.

The new residents
Cities provide new homes for many animals. In the search for food and security, they quickly adapt to their new surroundings.

Green corridors
A kestrel hovering above a road hunting for prey is an increasingly common sight. Roads and railway lines form "green corridors" which lead animals into town centers. The overgrown roadsides are perfect places for animals to find food and cover without the fear of being disturbed.

In the gardens
For many animals, gardens and parks offer a halfway house between country and city life. There is plenty of space, and shelter and food are easy to find. Insects abound for birds to eat, and owls and foxes prey on small animals, such as mice. Animals soon change their diet, especially when people put out food for them.

Insects in the home

The countryside teems with insects, but large numbers can also be found in towns and cities. Many, like moths and beetles, thrive in houses, feeding on food scraps, clothes and furniture.

A common pest found in the home is the carpet beetle. Its fluffy larvae are called woolly bears. They destroy carpets by eating the woolen fibers.

The tiny holes made by adult woodworm beetles and the telltale dust from their wood-boring larvae are sure signs of this widespread pest.

The clothes moth is another pest whose larvae eat natural fibers. It lays its eggs among woolen clothes which provide food for its caterpillars.

The death-watch beetle also eats wood, weakening beams and furniture. It gets its name from the eerie sound it makes as it thumps its head on the wood.

Garbage dumps

Garbage dumps are a major source of food for city animals. In North America raccoons raid trash cans and in Canada polar bears have been known to venture into towns to raid dumps. Scavenging gulls use discarded toothbrushes and hairpins to make nests. Some animals, like mice and rats, have become pests because they spread disease.

New homes

City buildings offer a wide choice of new homes for animals. Seabirds like herring gulls and oystercatchers build their nests on flat, pebble-dash roofs instead of cliffs. House martins and swifts nest in roof eaves, storks on chimney stacks, and barn owls in lofts and church belfries. Bats find plenty of space and warmth in the attics of houses, which replace their natural homes in caves and hollow trees.

Polar bear

Raccoon

31

LIFE ON THE RIVERBANK

Some of the world's most interesting animals and plants are found in or around rivers. Every river provides water, food and a home to a wide variety of wildlife. Throughout its length, however, a river is constantly changing. It may start its journey as a fast-moving, bubbling mountain brook, but by the time it reaches the sea it has grown much wider and calmer and flows more slowly.

Just as the river changes with each stage of its journey, so do its banks and the types of animals that live there. Water voles and kingfishers build

their tunnels in the sandbanks cut away by fast-moving water. The reed beds that grow beside slow-moving water, on the other hand, provide refuge and safe nesting places for water birds like the grebe and reed warbler.

The river itself is a complex world of its own, teeming with microscopic creatures, insect larvae and fish. All these provide ample food for insects patrolling the surface of the water in search of prey and for the birds and small animals that come to feed at the water's edge.

Common frog

Mayfly

Great crested grebes

Kingfisher

Water boatmen

Water snail

Sticklebacks

Mayfly
Mayflies swarm at the water's edge from May onward. Their larvae live underwater for two years. The adults mate the day they are born and die the evening of the same day.

Kingfisher
The brilliant colors of the kingfisher sparkle as it dives from its perch and plunges into the water to catch fish. It lays its eggs in tunnels that it digs in the riverbank.

Water boatmen
Water boatmen have strong hind legs which they use like oars to push them through the water in search of prey. They have wings too, so they are also able to fly.

Dipper
With its large, clawed feet, the dipper is an expert at walking on slippery rocks in the water. It walks upstream in fast-moving water, searching for fish and crayfish to eat.

A watery world

Early summer along a quiet stretch of the river brings many animals down to the riverbank. The birds are busy feeding their young and insects bask in the sunshine. The otter and kingfisher are on a constant lookout for food.

Reed warbler

Otter

Dipper

Dragonfly

Perch

Caddisfly larva

Dragonfly
Its huge eyes and four large wings make the dragonfly a fast and efficient hunter. It feeds on other insects that it catches as it flies up and down the river.

Otter
An excellent swimmer, the otter is well adapted to life in the water, with thick, waterproof fur and a long tail that it uses as a rudder. It feeds mainly on fish, but also on frogs and birds.

Water vole
This expert swimmer builds its nest in a tunnel system that it digs in the grassy bank near slow-moving water. Its burrows often have entrances both above and below water.

Caddisfly larva
Many caddisfly larvae make protective cases to live in. Some are made of pieces of stick or leaf, others out of tiny shells. Most of the larvae live and feed on the riverbed.

MARSHLANDS

Marshlands are strange places, half land and half water. Some of them are called marshes and others bogs, fens or swamps, but they all harbor an astonishing variety of wildlife. Some marshlands look like lakes, while others are covered with reed beds and look like grasslands, even though they are waterlogged for most of the year. There are both fresh- and saltwater marshes. The freshwater ones are usually found around the edges of lakes or ponds, or where a wide river floods its banks every year. Saltwater marshes are mostly in low-lying coastal areas near a river estuary.

The Everglades in the southern United States look like grasslands dotted with the occasional island of trees. In fact they are a vast marshland on either side of a wide, shallow, grassy river. As with many marshes, the water level in the Everglades rises and falls with the seasons, but all year round these semi-tropical marshes provide a home for all kinds of exotic animals.

A watery scene

The grasses, sedges and rushes of the Everglades provide a haven for great numbers of birds which roost in the reed beds. They also form an ideal hiding place for predators such as alligators, snakes and bobcats.

Green darner dragonfly

Everglades kite

Anhinga

Cotton mice

Largemouth bass

Bluegill

American alligator
American alligators are often found in deep pools known as "gator holes." These are always full of fish, and in the dry season many other water animals also take refuge there.

Everglades kite
Now protected in Florida, the Everglades kite has unusual feeding habits: it eats nothing but one type of water snail. It pries the snails out of their shells with its bill.

Florida turtle
Florida turtles are becoming more rare, as they have been hunted by collectors. In conservation areas, they thrive in lagoons where they eat plants along the banks.

Anhinga
Anhingas dive underwater to catch fish, spearing them with their sharp beaks. They are also known as "snakebirds" because they have very long, snakelike necks.

Snowy egret
Groups of snowy egrets stand in the shallow water to feed on frogs, fish and crayfish. With long legs and a long bill, egrets are perfectly adapted to life in the marshes.

Lilac-banded longtail
The lilac-banded longtail is purplish brown in color and prefers shade to open sunlight. This butterfly feeds on the nectar from flowers, but risks being eaten by birds and lizards.

Bobcat
Bobcats are North American lynxes. They hunt at night for birds, rabbits, cotton mice, rats and squirrels. They stalk their prey stealthily, then pounce on it.

Raccoon

Lilac-banded longtails

Purple gallinule

Great blue heron
The stately great blue heron stalks its prey of fish, insects and small reptiles along the water's edge. It stands very still, then lunges at its target with its long bill.

Alligator gar
Lurking in the reed beds, the alligator gar has a long, thin body and long jaws, perfectly shaped for moving through the reeds. It is very fierce and eats most other kinds of fish.

Purple gallinule
An expert at moving deftly from one floating leaf to another on its well-splayed toes, the purple gallinule feeds on seeds, fruit, leaves and insects. It is a good swimmer.

Cottonmouth moccasin
The deadly cottonmouth moccasin snake hunts its prey at night. It swims well, holding its head above water, ready to strike at small birds, frogs and other animals.

THE SMALLEST ANIMALS

Every branch of the animal kingdom has its midgets as well as its giants – animals that are unusually tiny and may even be too small to see with the naked eye. Nobody knows why some animals are so small. Many of them come from remote islands. Others live in dense forests where survival is perhaps easier for a small animal, which can move faster and hide more easily than a large one. The most numerous animals on earth are in fact the smallest of all – the insects and millions of microscopic creatures too small for us to see. Here we take a look at some of the tiniest animals.

True-to-life
All the animals shown here are drawn life-size. Each is one of the smallest animals of its type discovered so far.

A tiny primate
The lesser mouse lemur of Madagascar is one of the smallest primates (*see page 63*) in the world. It measures 12 inches (30 cm) from head to tail and weighs up to 2.8 ounces (80 g). It lives in dense forest and hunts for its food at night.

The smallest bird
The smallest bird in the world is the minuscule bee hummingbird, which lives in Cuba. Not much is known about it, but an adult male bird is only about 2¼ inches (5.7 cm) long and half of its length is taken up with its bill and tail alone.

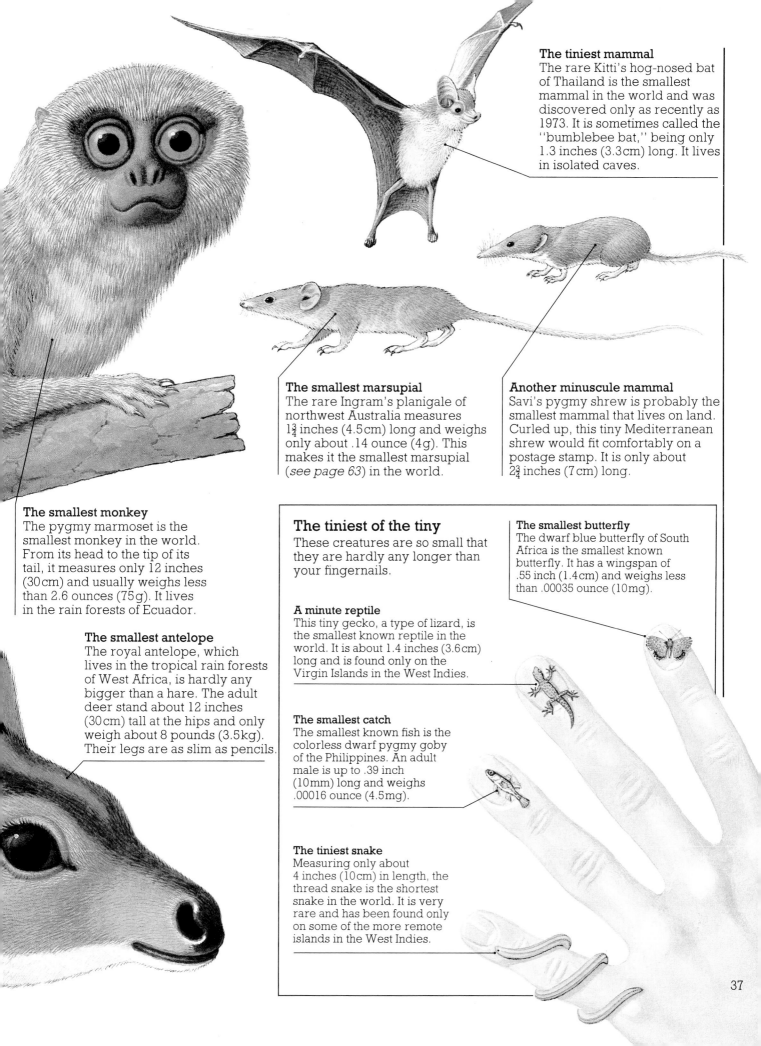

The tiniest mammal
The rare Kitti's hog-nosed bat of Thailand is the smallest mammal in the world and was discovered only as recently as 1973. It is sometimes called the "bumblebee bat," being only 1.3 inches (3.3cm) long. It lives in isolated caves.

The smallest marsupial
The rare Ingram's planigale of northwest Australia measures 1¾ inches (4.5cm) long and weighs only about .14 ounce (4g). This makes it the smallest marsupial (*see page 63*) in the world.

Another minuscule mammal
Savi's pygmy shrew is probably the smallest mammal that lives on land. Curled up, this tiny Mediterranean shrew would fit comfortably on a postage stamp. It is only about 2¾ inches (7cm) long.

The smallest monkey
The pygmy marmoset is the smallest monkey in the world. From its head to the tip of its tail, it measures only 12 inches (30cm) and usually weighs less than 2.6 ounces (75g). It lives in the rain forests of Ecuador.

The smallest antelope
The royal antelope, which lives in the tropical rain forests of West Africa, is hardly any bigger than a hare. The adult deer stand about 12 inches (30cm) tall at the hips and only weigh about 8 pounds (3.5kg). Their legs are as slim as pencils.

The tiniest of the tiny
These creatures are so small that they are hardly any longer than your fingernails.

A minute reptile
This tiny gecko, a type of lizard, is the smallest known reptile in the world. It is about 1.4 inches (3.6cm) long and is found only on the Virgin Islands in the West Indies.

The smallest catch
The smallest known fish is the colorless dwarf pygmy goby of the Philippines. An adult male is up to .39 inch (10mm) long and weighs .00016 ounce (4.5mg).

The tiniest snake
Measuring only about 4 inches (10cm) in length, the thread snake is the shortest snake in the world. It is very rare and has been found only on some of the more remote islands in the West Indies.

The smallest butterfly
The dwarf blue butterfly of South Africa is the smallest known butterfly. It has a wingspan of .55 inch (1.4cm) and weighs less than .00035 ounce (10mg).

THE GREAT GRASSLANDS

More than a quarter of all the land on Earth is covered with grass, and most of the continents have vast grasslands that spread for thousands of miles. Different countries have different names for their grasslands. In North America they are called prairies and in South America pampas; in Central Asia there are steppes and the grassy plains of East Africa are called savannahs.

The great grasslands of the world are all in areas where few trees grow, either because there is not enough rain for them or because the ground is too dry and sandy. Grasses are very tough. They carry on growing after flood, fire or drought and can withstand constant grazing by animals. Because of this, they provide a continuous food supply for great numbers of plant-eating animals, many of which have become specially adapted to feeding on them. Here and on the next two pages you can see some of the animals, both large and small, that live on the wide plains of the African savannah.

The savannah of East Africa
On the savannah, seas of open grassland are dotted with the occasional thorn bush and acacia tree. More groups of large animals live on these grassy plains than anywhere else in the world.

Lions
Lions live in groups called prides, led by a dominant male. Most of the hunting is done by lionesses, often as a team. They creep up on their victims – zebras and antelopes – then give chase.

Hyenas
Hyenas are a type of wild dog and hunt at night in packs. They single out a victim from a herd of wildebeests or zebras and chase it until it tires, then tear it to pieces.

Giraffes
The giraffe's enormous height enables it to eat the leaves at the tops of trees which other browsing animals cannot reach, so it usually has a plentiful supply of food.

Elephants
Herds of elephants move slowly across the savannah, browsing and grazing. In the dry season they often travel, or migrate, long distances in search of fresh pastures.

Hyenas

Vultures

Vultures
Vultures soar at great heights above the African plains, searching for an abandoned kill. Once they have sighted a carcass, they land in droves to feed on the remains.

Eland
Many types of antelopes roam the savannah. The eland is the largest of them. Like other antelopes and hoofed animals, elands graze in large herds, seeking safety in numbers.

Wildebeests

Wildebeests live in huge herds, often several thousand strong. The whole herd migrates vast distances when the dry season starts, in search of water and fresh pastures.

Weaver bird colonies

Because trees on the savannah are scattered, whole flocks of gregarious weaver birds weave their elaborate basket-shaped nests in the same thorn bush or tree.

Weaver birds

Wildebeests

Zebras

Leopard

Thompson's gazelles

Zebras

Zebras live in herds, often close to herds of wildebeests. Their main enemy is the lion, and some people think the zebra's stripes help to confuse lions when they give chase.

Thomson's gazelles

The Thomson's gazelle is more numerous than any other gazelle on the savannah. When being pursued by a predator, it twists and turns to try to escape its attacker.

Rhinoceros

There are two types of African rhino – the black one, which feeds on leaves and twigs, and the white one, which eats mainly grass. The rhino uses its horns to defend itself.

Leopard

The leopard hunts on its own, and its spots help to camouflage it as it stalks its prey. It uses a tree as its ''pantry,'' carrying its kill up onto a branch, out of reach of scavengers.

Forest of grass

A closer look at the savannah scene on the previous pages reveals another, hidden world of animals. Among the tall clumps of grass and plants live birds, lizards, snakes and thousands of tiny, scurrying insects. To these animals, the stalks of grass are like a tall, dense forest where they live, breed and take refuge.

Secretary bird

Banded mongoose

Zebras

Ants

Banded mongoose
The mongoose is a formidable snake-killer. It relies on its speed and agility to avoid a snake's poisonous fangs. Mongooses also eat birds' eggs, lizards and small mammals.

Common agama
This small lizard lives in groups of up to 25 members and forages for insects like grasshoppers and locusts. The female lays her eggs in the warm soil in the rainy season.

Grasshopper
The grasshopper is one of the most common grassland insects and is eaten by many other animals. It uses its long back legs to leap away from danger.

Puff adder
The puff adder is one of the grasslands' most dangerous predators. Camouflaged in the grass, it lies in wait for its prey and strikes with its long, poisonous fangs.

Termite mound

Bee

Grasshopper

Termites
Tiny termites, or "white ants," are master builders. Their earth mounds, often several yards high, have chambers for their leaders. They may house over a million termites.

Locusts
A swarm of locusts contains up to 10,000 million insects, which need 3 tons of food a day. Locusts can destroy a field of crops and are a menace to farmers .

Dung beetles
Dung beetles make small balls out of animal dung and then find a suitable place to bury them. They lay their eggs in the dung, which will provide food for the emerging larvae.

Ant lion
Ant lion larvae trap their prey in small, conical pits they dig in the loose, sandy soil. They lie in wait at the bottom of the pit, ready to snap up small insects that tumble in.

41

HUNTERS AND THE HUNTED

All animals need a regular supply of food. Plant-eaters have to eat a lot and spend most of their time grazing and browsing. When they have eaten all the food in one area, they move on to another. Meat-eaters eat other animals, so they have to be efficient hunters to survive. The animals they hunt, however, have to be able to fend them off or to escape, so that *they* survive. The relationship between the hunter and the hunted is constantly changing. Sometimes the hunter wins and catches its prey; at other times the prey manages to escape from the hunter.

Every predator has its own method of hunting. Some hunt on their own; others in packs. Some chase their victims; others ambush them or lay traps for them. The animals they hunt use all kinds of tricks to confuse their enemies, as they are often unable to defend themselves. Here you can find out about some of the widely varying techniques of attack and defense carried out by the hunters and the animals they hunt.

A swift-footed hunter
A cheetah springs forward into a herd of wildebeests. They flee in all directions, twisting, turning and kicking, in an attempt to confuse their pursuer and throw it off track.

Deadly attackers
Animals have perfected countless different ways of catching their prey. Some chase prey, but others use more devious methods:

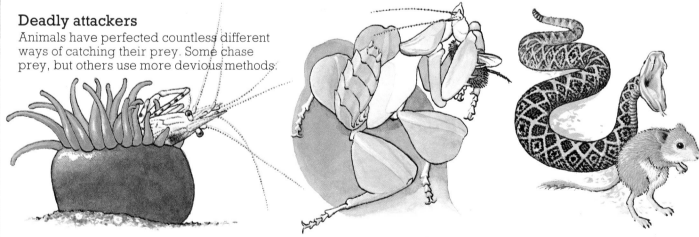

Stinging tentacles
The sea anemone stuns its prey with its stinging, poisonous tentacles. Its tentacles then close around the paralyzed prey and draw it down into the sea anemone's mouth.

A deadly disguise
This mantis is exactly the same color as the flower on which it is sitting. Perfectly camouflaged, it lies in wait of unsuspecting insects that visit the flower.

Poisonous fangs
The rattlesnake has needle-sharp, poisonous fangs. When it senses prey, it glides silently forward, then strikes swiftly, sinking its fangs deep into its victim.

Keeping watch
Wildebeests seek safety in numbers by moving around in vast herds. They keep a constant lookout for danger as they graze on the savannah, frequently lifting their heads to look around. It is hard for a predator to creep up on them unseen.

The hunter
The cheetah relies on its speed to catch prey and can run at up to 60 miles per hour (100kph) over short distances. It selects an animal from a herd, then creeps up as close as possible to its victim and suddenly sprints forward at lightning speed.

The chase
The herd scatters, but the cheetah pursues its victim. Unable to keep up speed for long, the cheetah catches its prey only if it can keep up with it for the first few hundred yards. It then brings the animal down and bites its throat to kill it.

Avoiding tactics
Not all animals run away from their predators. Some try to frighten attackers away and others use tricks to bluff the enemy.

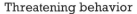

Faking injury
The ringed plover leads predators away from its young by pretending to have a broken wing and moving away from its nest. A safe distance away, it flies up and escapes.

All puffed up
When threatened, the puffer fish swallows water so that it looks twice its normal size. Its body swells into a balloon shape and all its spines stick out, putting off its enemy.

Threatening behavior
The frilled lizard of Australia tries to frighten off attackers by hissing and spreading its huge, frilled "collar," to make it look bigger and more fierce than it really is.

THE STEAMING JUNGLE

Rain forests or jungles are dense, steamy forests that grow in the tropics near the equator, where it is very hot and rains nearly every day.

The trees and plants grow very fast, competing with each other for light, and reach enormous heights, spreading out their branches and leaves like green parasols at the top. Ordinary plants grow to the size of trees, and the trees themselves are among the tallest in the world. There are no seasons in the jungle. It is hot all year round.

Jungles harbor the greatest variety of plants and animals in the world. These live at different levels in the trees, as in a multistory building, each level being completely different from the others. The jungle floor is mostly dark and gloomy. It is very hot and the air is still. Higher up, creepers called lianas hang like thick ropes between the towering tree trunks. Most of the animals in the jungle live at the very tops of the trees, about 150 feet (45m) above the ground, in the "canopy," where there is plenty of sunlight, and leaves, flowers and fruit to feed on.

On these two pages you can see the animals that live at ground level in the Amazon jungle of South America, the largest jungle in the world, and on the next two pages you can discover what life is like up in the canopy, high in the treetops.

Deep in the Amazon

The Amazon jungle is intersected by the Amazon River and thousands of smaller rivers. Shafts of sunlight reach the ground where a river breaks the wall of trees. Many reptiles and fish live in the murky waters, and other birds and animals come to feed and drink at the water's edge.

Anteater
Anteaters feed on termites and ants. They rip open the nests of their prey with their long claws, and lick up the insects with their 2-foot (60-cm) tongues, which are coated with sticky saliva.

Caiman
Caimans are relatives of the alligator. They live close to the river, snapping up unwary small animals and birds that come to drink at the water's edge. They can lay up to 30 eggs at a time.

Anaconda
The largest living snake, the anaconda attacks birds and animals that come to the river to drink. It winds its body around its prey, squeezes it to death, then swallows it whole.

Arrau turtle
The Arrau turtle is one of the largest turtles on Earth. The heavy female turtles haul themselves out onto the sandbanks to lay their eggs. They can lay up to 150 eggs each year.

Hatchetfish

Neon tetra fish

Electric eel

Manatee
The timid manatee, or sea cow, rests under the water by day, rising only to breathe. It feeds on plants, tearing them up from the riverbed with its strong upper lip.

Army ants

Morpho butterflies

Hoatzins
The odd-looking hoatzin is not very good at flying and prefers to clamber around trees. The baby birds have claws on their wings to help them grip onto branches as they climb trees.

Scarlet ibis

Arrau turtle

Arapaima

Hatchetfish
The hatchetfish of the Amazon are the world's only true flying fish. They can actually flap their outstretched fins and "fly" above the water in pursuit of airborne insects.

Capybaras
Capybaras are the largest rodents (*see page 63*) on Earth – the size of pigs. Their feet are partially webbed. They spend most of their time in the river, feeding on plants.

Piranhas
Very ferocious, piranhas hunt in shoals of several hundred. They tear the flesh from their prey with their sharp teeth. Strangely, some types of piranhas eat only plants.

Jaguar
The mottled coat of the jaguar camouflages it as it stalks its prey through the dimly lit trees. It is the largest cat in South America and is able both to climb trees and to swim.

THE TREETOP CANOPY

Unlike woodland trees, jungle trees have no branches low down. They start branching about 100 feet (30m) from the ground, providing a dense canopy of branches and leaves. This tangled world of trees, orchids, ferns and other plants is home to a wide variety of insects, snakes, animals and birds which can cope with living high above the ground. Birds, monkeys and sloths grip tightly to the branches as they forage for luscious fruits, flowers, leaves and berries.

Howler monkey
Feeding by day on leaves and fruit, howler monkeys move deftly through the canopy. The males loudly defend their territory – their roaring voices can be heard 2 miles (3km) away.

Sloth
Living and sleeping upside down, the sloth has hooklike claws that grip tightly as it inches its way slowly along the branches of a tree. It feeds on leaves and buds.

Gibbon

Sloth

Tree boa

Tree porcupine

Tree porcupine
The tree porcupine uses its tail, as well as its hands and feet, to help it grip tightly onto branches. Despite its protective quills, the porcupine is preyed on by eagles.

Tree boa
Hidden in the leaves, the emerald tree boa camouflages itself by pressing its body close to the branch. It strikes at its prey to catch it, then squeezes it to death.

Harpy eagle
Harpy eagles are the feared predators of the canopy. They chase their prey at speeds of 50 miles per hour (80kph), and pluck monkeys from the trees with their claws.

Spider monkey
The most agile of monkeys, spider monkeys swing from branch to branch through the canopy. They use their long and very strong tails to grip onto branches.

Toucan
When asleep, a toucan lays its rainbow-colored bill along its back, and covers the bill with its tail. It uses its incredible bill to pick fruit and berries and toss them down its throat.

Frilled coquette hummingbird

Ruby topaz hummingbird

Macaw
Macaws are the largest of the South American parrots. They have vice-like feet for gripping onto branches and strong hooked beaks for cracking open nuts to eat.

Butterflies
There is a greater variety of butterflies in the jungle than anywhere else in the world. Their dazzling colors help to camouflage them when they alight on brightly colored flowers.

Hummingbird
Glossy hummingbirds hover in front of flowers as if suspended in midair. They probe inside the flowers for nectar with their long tongues, pollinating them as they do so.

Tree frog
A huge variety of tree frogs spend their entire lives high in the trees. Some live in the water that collects in the center of plants growing on lofty tree branches.

47

CAMOUFLAGE AND SIGNALLING

All animals have a strong natural instinct for survival and many of them have adapted to their habitats in very clever ways. Many animals need to be as inconspicuous as possible most of the time, so that they are not spotted by hungry predators. Constantly running away or looking for hiding places takes up a lot of time, so some animals have developed cunning forms of camouflage, which make them very hard to see. The colors and patterns of their coats, feathers or skin match their surroundings so well that they become almost invisible.

Camouflage is not the only way in which animals make use of color and pattern. Some animals are brilliantly colored and actually show off their colors as much as possible, even to their enemies. Their bright colors are used to proclaim who they are, are flaunted by males as a challenge to other males and are shown off to attract a mate. Sometimes certain combinations of bright colors, such as yellow and black, or red and black, show that an animal is poisonous and has to be avoided at all costs.

Color and pattern are both used as a means of signalling, but animals have other ways of passing on messages to each other too. Here you can find out more about types of camouflage and signalling in the animal world.

Showing off
Male birds use all sorts of tricks to attract a mate. Many of them are brilliantly colored and show off their feathers or perform elaborate courtship dances to win a female's attention.

Frigate birds

Camouflage artists

Animal camouflage can take many forms. One of the most common is for an animal to have a mottled coat or feathers with patches of dark and light coloring. This makes the animal hard to see against a background of rocks or sun-dappled foliage, especially when it keeps quite still. Other animals, such as some insects, look like part of the plant on which they live. One of the best camouflage artists of all is the chameleon, a type of lizard, which changes color to match its surroundings.

The Texas horned lizard matches the stony desert ground on which it lives so well that when it stands still it is almost invisible. Its camouflage enables it to lie in wait for unsuspecting birds and small animals that come close, then it attacks them.

The leaf insects of the Tropics mimic the colors and the shapes of the leaves among which they live. They do this so successfully that they would never be able to move to another type of plant, as they would be spotted by a predator instantly.

The plaice is very hard to detect as it lies on the seabed. It can change its color and pattern to match its background perfectly. Its body can flatten out to hug the surface of the sand or rocks it lies on, so both its eyes are on the top side of its head.

A dazzling display

The male birds of paradise of Papua New Guinea perform courtship dances on a tree branch to win a mate. The drab-looking females choose the males with the most dazzling plumage and dance.

Birds of paradise

Passing on messages

Animals do not always communicate with each other by sound. They can pass messages to each other by means of color and behavior.

The ring-tailed lemurs of Madagascar spend almost as much time on the ground as they do in the trees. They pass signals to each other by waving their long, banded black-and-white tails, which give off scent from their scent glands.

The spectacular colors of this South American frog warn potential predators that it is highly poisonous. The poison that the frog secretes in slime from its skin is lethal enough to paralyze a bird or a small monkey within minutes.

Macaw

A courtship dance

Gannets always recognize each other in the crowded colonies where they live, because each one has slightly different markings. Courting pairs perform dances where each movement and step has a special meaning.

Gannets

A magnificent chest

During courtship, the male frigate bird tries to impress the female by inflating his bright scarlet throat pouch into a kind of balloon. The female shows her interest in him by rubbing her head against his spectacular chest.

Lorikeet

Gaudy birds

The macaws of South America and the lorikeets of Australia, New Zealand and the Pacific Islands live in noisy flocks high up in the rain forests. Their brilliant colors help them to recognize each other.

49

THE BURNING DESERT

Deserts are the driest places on Earth. In parts of them it may not rain for many years. Some deserts are vast expanses of sand; others are rocky or covered with thin scrub. Some of them, like the Gobi Desert in Asia, are cold in the winter, but many of them are hot all year round. Temperatures soar to great heights during the day, then may often drop to well below freezing at night.

Deserts often look dead, as if nothing grows or lives there, but many amazing plants and animals have adapted to life in the harsh conditions. Desert plants have long roots and tough skins. They flower and seed the moment there is rain. Desert animals have unique ways of coping without much water. On the next four pages you can find out about life in two different kinds of deserts.

The biggest desert on Earth
The Sahara stretches right across northern Africa. Most of the animals that live there shelter from the burning heat during the day and emerge only to hunt for food as the sun sinks in the sky.

Surviving the desert
These three desert animals have developed especially clever ways of coping with the intense heat and lack of water.

Dromedary camel
The camel is the largest animal in the desert. It can survive for weeks without water, living on the food stored as fat in its hump and on water stored in its stomach. The camel can cope with intense heat, as its large body heats up slowly and it does not have to sweat much to keep cool. Its feet splay out as it walks, so it does not sink into the sand, and during sandstorms it can close its nostrils to keep out sand.

Lanner falcon
The lanner falcon soars over the desert by day, searching for small animals to eat. It swoops down on its prey, seizing it in its sharp talons, and tears it apart with its hooked bill.

Lanner falcon

Gecko
The gecko is a type of lizard that can skim across the sand. It has webbed toes, which stop it from sinking, and which it uses like shovels to help it burrow beneath the sand.

Gerbils
The hopping, mouselike gerbil ventures from its burrow at dusk to feed. It gets all the liquid it needs from the seeds and grasses it eats, and it is hunted by the fennec fox.

Sidewinder snake

Fennec fox

Gerbils

Sidewinder snake
Slithering over hot sand can make snakes too hot. The sidewinder moves forward in a wavelike motion, lifting part of its body above the sand as it does so to help it keep cool. It leaves a mark on the sand as it goes.

Fennec fox
The fennec fox's giant ears work rather like radiators. They give off heat to help keep the fox cool. They also enable it to detect sounds made by the small birds and animals it hunts when it emerges from its burrow at dusk.

Scorpion
Scorpions use the venomous stingers in their tails mainly to defend themselves. They catch insects and spiders in their giant pincers, then tear them apart to eat them.

African sand grouse
The sand grouse flies great distances to the nearest water hole to get water for its chicks. It soaks its breast feathers, then flies back to its chicks, who suck the water out.

Addax
The addax antelope has wide hoofs that help it to move easily across the sand. It does not drink any water at all, but gets all the liquid it needs from the plants it eats.

Locusts
Locusts, desert relatives of grasshoppers, lay their eggs in warm sand. They swarm in millions, eating thousands of tons of plants before moving on to a new area.

Scorpion

THE NORTH AMERICAN DESERT

The North American deserts lie in the southwest part of the United States. Here the summers are hot and the winters are cold – snow may even fall. These deserts are not sandy landscapes with huge dunes. Parts of them are stony and bare, dotted with rocks and hills that have been worn into strange shapes by the wind. Other areas are covered with low-lying scrub and thorn bushes.

The best-known of the American desert plants are the cacti. Like many other desert plants, they can store water. When it rains, their widespread roots suck up water and their stems swell to store it. Other plants also come to life when it rains. Seeds that may have been lying dormant for years suddenly sprout, flower and make new seeds, briefly turning the desert into a meadow.

The desert at night
As night falls, the desert comes to life. Kangaroo rats emerge from their burrows, and spiders and scorpions appear from beneath rocks, as all the animals start their search for food.

Adapting to life in the desert
Each of these three animals has its own way of avoiding the heat and conserving liquid in the harsh desert conditions.

Kangaroo rat
The kangaroo rat keeps cool during the day by staying in its burrow, the mouth of which it plugs up to keep the air inside cool and moist. Like the gerbil of the Sahara, this rat gets all the liquid it needs from the seeds it eats.

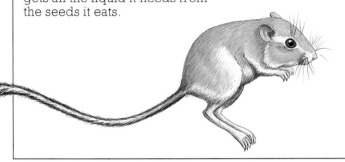

Whippoorwill
The whippoorwill's coloring helps to camouflage it in rocky areas. It avoids the cold of the winter by hibernating, waking in spring when there are more insects to eat.

Rattlesnake
The rattlesnake is poisonous and shakes the rattle on its tail as a warning if a big animal comes too near. It hunts small animals, killing them with its poisonous fangs.

Chuckwalla
The chuckwalla lizard hides under a rock during the night and comes out to bask in the sun in the morning. A plant-eater, this lizard stores water in folds of skin on its sides.

Gila monster
This bulky lizard is poisonous, and its bright colors act as a warning to predators. It eats bird and lizard eggs and stores fat in its thick tail, for times of food shortage.

Jackrabbit

Coyote

Gila monster

Roadrunner
The roadrunner rarely flies, but it can run very fast. It chases after insects and lizards and even kills snakes, jabbing at them with its sharp beak. It sits on its eggs to keep them cool, rather than warm, using its tail as a sunshade.

Brazilian free-tailed bats

Gila woodpecker
Desert birds have to shield their eggs from the sun, as well as from predators. Gila woodpeckers often nest in holes they make in the giant saguaro cacti of the Sonoran Desert.

Spade-foot toad
Spade-foot toads mate and lay eggs as soon as it rains. When the soil begins to dry, they dig themselves into the ground with their spade-like hind feet. They seal themselves in burrows and wait for about nine months, until it rains next.

Elf owl
The elf owl is one of the smallest of all owls. It roosts in cacti, using the abandoned nests of Gila woodpeckers, and emerges at night to feed on insects such as beetles and moths.

Tarantula
People think the tarantula is dangerous, but its poison is deadly only for insects and birds. This spider hunts at night, seizing its prey with its pincers, then giving it a fatal bite.

Kit fox
The kit fox is similar to the fennec fox of the Sahara (*see page 51*). Like the fennec, it has large ears and good hearing. It lives in a burrow and hunts small animals at night.

Kit fox

Striped skunk

Kangaroo rats

Tarantula

Scorpion

THE BURROWERS

Not all animals spend their lives out in the open. Some of them dig burrows and spend part or all of their time underground, where predators cannot reach them and they can bring up their young safely. A burrow can provide protection from the sun in hot places or a sheltered spot to hibernate in cold places. Burrows may be dug in soil, sand or snow. Some burrowers live almost permanently underground; others just use their burrow as a retreat. Most burrowing animals have thick, warm fur, strong claws for digging and streamlined bodies, so they can move easily under the ground.

Badgers
With strong front claws and powerful bodies, badgers are well designed for burrowing. Their setts, usually no more than 6½ feet (2m) below ground, may be used by different badgers for centuries.

Moles
Moles are master burrowers, using their large front paws like spades. They are very nearsighted, but have whiskers on their faces for feeling their way underground.

Earthworms
As many as 500 worms may live in one square yard of soil. They make their tunnels by pushing and eating their way through the soil. Tiny hairs on their bodies stop them from slipping as they dig.

Burrowing owl
Empty prairie dog burrows are often used as nests by the burrowing owls of the American prairies. The owls use their large claws to make the holes bigger, and feed their young on insects.

Moles

Earthworms

Life underground
Here you can see different burrowers in their homes. All of them burrow in soil, but you would never normally find them together, as they come from different places all around the world.

Pink fairy armadillo
This South American armadillo spends most of its life underground. It ventures outside only at night to hunt for insects. It makes its burrow by digging with its front legs and pushing with its snout.

Rabbits
A large rabbit warren may house 400 rabbits and have over 2,000 entrances. Different tunnels act as roadways, bedrooms and nurseries. Rabbits also use small burrows and even old foxholes as homes.

Prairie dogs
Several thousand prairie dogs may live together as a "township." If there is danger, they let out high-pitched barks to warn the others to dive underground.

Trap-door spider
The trap-door spider digs a deep tunnel in the soil and covers the entrance with a fine silk web and moss. As an unsuspecting insect walks across it, the spider lifts up its trap-door and grabs its prey.

Prairie dogs

Rabbits

THE OCEAN DEPTHS

The seas and oceans are the largest natural habitat, covering over two-thirds of the Earth. The oceans are vast and varied. The seabed has a landscape more dramatic than dry land, with towering mountains and deep, dark chasms. In places the mountains are so high that they form islands above the surface of the water. The oceans are, however, still mostly unknown. They are among the last places left on Earth that humans have not really explored, and there are probably many animals living there yet to be discovered.

A huge variety of creatures live in the oceans, varying in size from microscopic plankton to the blue whale. Most animals live in the sunlit surface waters of the sea, where plant food is plentiful. This is grazed by large shoals of small fish, which are hunted in turn by larger fish. Several miles below, however, the waters are pitch dark and freezing cold. No plants can grow at this depth, yet numerous strange fish flourish there, many of them providing their own light with a weird array of luminous spines and fins.

A world on different levels
This imaginary scene shows some of the animals that live at different levels in the ocean – from the shoals of small fish that live in the warm surface waters to the grotesque-looking creatures that lurk in the murky depths far below.

Man-of-war
Beneath its float, which acts like a sail, the Portuguese man-of-war trails deadly, stinging tentacles through the water. These paralyze and kill unsuspecting fish that swim into them.

Tuna
Streamlined, with spindle-shaped bodies and forked tails, tuna are high-speed swimmers that travel great distances. Their main sources of food are squids and smaller fish.

Squids
Squids are very fast swimmers and move forward or backward with equal ease. They have a horny beak, ten tentacles with suckers, and the largest known eyes of any animal in the world.

Hatchetfish
These tiny deep-sea fish have transparent fins and telescopic eyes that point upward. Their bodies are flattened from side to side and they have rows of lights on their undersides.

A world in miniature
The seas are full of tiny drifting plants called *phytoplankton*. These are an astonishing variety of shapes, but they are so small they can be seen only under a microscope. Most of them live in the top 330 feet (100m) of water, where sunlight can reach them and they can grow. Feeding on these tiny plants are minuscule drifting creatures called *zooplankton*. The two types of plankton are the main food supply of many sea creatures. Even the blue whale feeds on some types of plankton, sieving it from the water.

Manta ray
A giant, diamond-shaped fish, the manta ray can measure up to 20 feet (6m) from the tip of one fin to the other. It flaps its way through the sunlit water, feeding on plankton.

Dolphins
Like whales, dolphins are not fish but mammals. They swim in groups called schools and navigate like bats, producing high-pitched sounds that bounce off obstacles.

Sardines
Vast shoals of sardines move through the upper waters of the ocean. They try to confuse pursuing predators, such as tuna, by scattering in many different directions.

Hammerhead shark
Sharks detect prey by scent. The nostrils of this fierce hunter are on the ends of its hammer-shaped head. When it smells prey, it swings its head from side to side to locate it.

Pilot whale
Pilot whales are large dolphins which may be up to 30 feet (9m) long. They swim in schools several hundred strong, led by a leader, or "pilot." They are sometimes stranded on land.

Conger eel
The conger has a long scaleless body. Usually found in shallow waters, it migrates to deeper waters to spawn. The larvae drift in the sea for one to two years before becoming eels.

Lantern fish

Anglerfish
The deep-sea anglerfish attracts prey by means of a light dangling in front of it on the end of its long spine like a fishing rod. When small fish come too close, the anglerfish eats them.

Viperfish
Another deep-sea fish, the viperfish gets its name from its snakelike body and sharp, poison-filled fangs. It has rows of lights along its body and inside its mouth.

57

THE LIFE OF THE CORAL REEF

Coral reefs are among the wonders of the natural world, forming brilliantly colored underwater kingdoms inhabited by vast numbers of exotic creatures and plants. They grow only in warm tropical waters shallow enough for the sun to reach them. Muddy or polluted water kills them.

The reefs take thousands of years to form and are built entirely by tiny creatures no more than a half inch long. These creatures, called *coral polyps*, are similar to sea anemones. They grow joined together in huge colonies. There are thousands of different types of coral. Some look like flowers or tiny trees, others like ferns or sponges. Each coral polyp grows a protective limestone casing. When corals die, the casings are left behind and build up to form a reef on which new corals grow. A reef grows incredibly slowly, about a half inch a year, but it can grow to a spectacular size. The Great Barrier Reef, which is the biggest reef of all, stretches for about 1,250 miles (2,000 km) along the northeastern coast of Australia and can be seen from the moon.

An underwater kingdom
Like an enormous, sunlit kingdom, the coral reef provides a home of magical beauty for thousands of brightly colored plants and animals. Many of the creatures have developed unique relationships with each other and help to feed or protect their partner.

Warning colors
The alarming-looking dragonfish has poison in the spines of its fins. Its bright colors warn other fish that it is poisonous. If threatened, it jabs an enemy with its spines.

Butterfly fish

Copper-banded butterfly fish

Imperial angelfish

Family colors
Many of the fish that live on the reef are brilliantly colored and patterned. Each species of fish has its own "family colors," so that it can be easily recognized both by other fish and by members of its own species, or family.

A borrowed home
The hermit crab makes its home in an old seashell. It carries sea anemones around on the shell. These feed on the crab's leftovers and in return protect the crab with their stinging tentacles.

Dragonfish

Fan coral

Brain coral

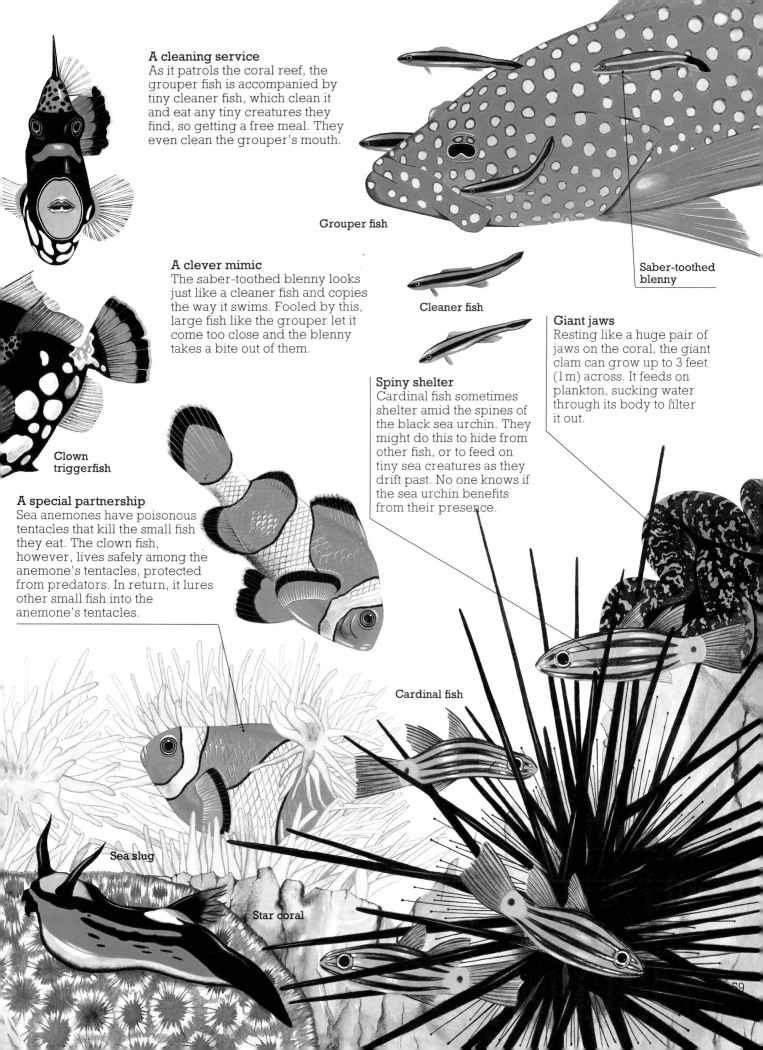

A cleaning service
As it patrols the coral reef, the grouper fish is accompanied by tiny cleaner fish, which clean it and eat any tiny creatures they find, so getting a free meal. They even clean the grouper's mouth.

Grouper fish

Saber-toothed blenny

A clever mimic
The saber-toothed blenny looks just like a cleaner fish and copies the way it swims. Fooled by this, large fish like the grouper let it come too close and the blenny takes a bite out of them.

Cleaner fish

Giant jaws
Resting like a huge pair of jaws on the coral, the giant clam can grow up to 3 feet (1 m) across. It feeds on plankton, sucking water through its body to filter it out.

Clown triggerfish

Spiny shelter
Cardinal fish sometimes shelter amid the spines of the black sea urchin. They might do this to hide from other fish, or to feed on tiny sea creatures as they drift past. No one knows if the sea urchin benefits from their presence.

A special partnership
Sea anemones have poisonous tentacles that kill the small fish they eat. The clown fish, however, lives safely among the anemone's tentacles, protected from predators. In return, it lures other small fish into the anemone's tentacles.

Cardinal fish

Sea slug

Star coral

ANIMALS IN DANGER

Animals are well adapted to natural habitats and for millions of years their numbers have been regulated by the forces of nature. People have changed all that. By destroying natural habitats, we have endangered the lives of many animals and plants. Unable to adapt to new conditions, many of them have become extinct; that is, they have died out completely and no longer exist.

People have cut down rain forests, used land for farming and built towns, thus destroying many natural habitats. Explorers have opened up areas where animals were once safe from harm, large cats have been killed for their fur and whales hunted to the point of near extinction. Lakes, rivers and the seas have been polluted, and all the time animals are being trapped and sold to wildlife collectors, zoos and research centers.

Some animals are now officially protected and cannot legally be trapped or killed without permission. Others live in safety in nature preserves or zoos. But unless people stop destroying natural habitats, there will be fewer and fewer places for animals to live, and fewer animals as a result.

Manatee
The gentle manatee is one of the last survivors of a large family of mammals that lived entirely in water. It is very nearsighted and has been widely hunted for its meat.

Manatee

Quetzal

Quetzal
The quetzal lives in the rain forests of Central America. Prized by the Mayan and Aztec Indians for its tail feathers, it has been hunted by collectors and is now very rare.

Przewalski's horse

California condor

Extinct animals
Possibly more species of animals have become extinct because of people than have died out naturally before people began to destroy their habitats and kill animals for their skin, fur or meat. In the rain forests alone, hundreds of species have become extinct, and thousands more are now at risk.

Dodo

The trusting dodo
Flightless and tame, the dodo was slaughtered for food by sailors on the island of Mauritius. Within 200 years of its discovery it was completely extinct.

Great auk
Great auks lived in the North Atlantic until about 1852. Clumsy on land, they were battered to death for their fat, meat and feathers.

Passenger pigeon

Passenger pigeon
Flocks of 2,000 million passenger pigeons used to be seen in North America. Because of shooting and snaring by people, they were extinct by 1914.

Great auk

Przewalski's horse
This is the last true wild horse, and it used to roam the desolate plains of central China and Mongolia in large herds. It has been saved from extinction by being bred in captivity in zoos.

California condor
Destruction of its habitat, shooting and pollution have made California condors nearly extinct. Only three birds are still known to exist in the wild, despite attempts to breed condors in captivity.

Blue whale

Giant panda
There are only about 800 to 1,000 giant pandas left in the wild, living in remote areas of China. They eat nothing but bamboo, and every 50 years the bamboo dies off mysteriously, causing many pandas to die.

Blue whale
In the 1930s, there were over 200,000 blue whales, but they were hunted for whale oil and their numbers dropped to fewer than 2,000. Now protected, they number at least 6,000.

Spanish lynx
This lynx used to be widespread in Spain, but much of the forest where it lived has been destroyed. There are now only about 15 pairs left and they live in remote mountainous areas.

Java rhinoceros
Today, there are fewer than 30 Java rhinos in existence, because of hunting and destruction of the rain forest on the over-populated island of Java. The Java rhino is now being bred in zoos.

Spanish lynx

Gorilla

Java rhinoceros

Gorilla
The largest of the apes, gorillas live in the tropical forests of central Africa. Their habitat is gradually being destroyed as the forests are cut down and taken over for farming.

Giant panda

Caspian tiger
The Caspian tiger lived mainly in dense woodlands along river valleys in central Russia. Most of these valleys have been destroyed by land reclamation schemes, and this tiger is now very rare as a result.

Green turtle
Once common in warm, tropical waters, the green turtle has been persecuted for its eggs, shell and meat. A turtle ranch on Bali is reintroducing the species to the wild.

Green turtle

Kiwi
The kiwi is related to the flightless birds called moas that once lived in New Zealand. It has been a protected species since 1896, but it is hunted by rats and domestic cats.

Kiwi

Caspian tiger

WHAT'S WHAT IN THE ANIMAL WORLD

There are so many different types of animals on Earth – over 10 million *species* or types – that naturalists have divided them up into different groups to make it easier to work out how they are related to each other. All the members of each group have one feature or more in common with each other – a backbone, for example, or a backbone and the same number of legs. Some groups are subdivided into smaller groups too. Here you can find out about the main groups of animals.

Invertebrates

All animals are classified according to whether or not they have a backbone. Invertebrates are animals without a backbone. Some, like jellyfish, have soft bodies. Others, like insects, have hard, outer skeletons. Insects, arachnids, crustaceans and mollusks are four different groups of invertebrates.

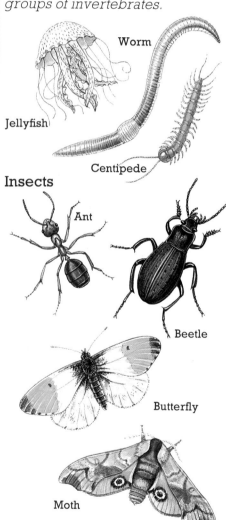

Jellyfish
Worm
Centipede

Insects

Ant
Beetle
Butterfly
Moth

Insects are the largest group of animals on Earth and live everywhere. They have six legs and a body divided into three parts. Most of them have one or two pairs of wings. Ants, beetles, flies and butterflies are all insects.

Arachnids

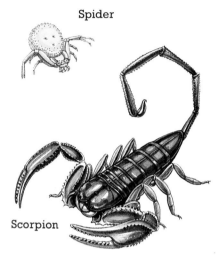

Spider
Scorpion

Arachnids have eight legs (two more than insects) and a hard, outer skeleton. Their bodies are usually in two parts. Most arachnids are hunters and live on land. They include spiders, scorpions, harvestmen and mites.

Crustaceans

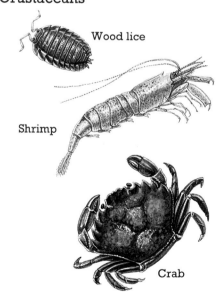

Wood lice
Shrimp
Crab

Most crustaceans live in water, especially in the sea, like crabs, lobsters and shrimps. Some, however, like wood lice, live in damp places on land. They all have bodies covered with a hard shell, sometimes in jointed plates.

Mollusks

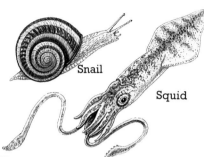

Snail
Squid

Slugs, snails, cockles and squids are all mollusks. They have soft bodies and sometimes a hard, protective shell, but unlike crustaceans, they don't have legs. They live mostly in water and are the second largest group of animals after the insects.

Vertebrates

Vertebrates are animals with a backbone and an internal skeleton. There are 46,000 known species of vertebrates and naturalists have divided them into five main groups: fish, amphibians, reptiles, birds and mammals. More than half of the different species of vertebrates known are fish.

Fish

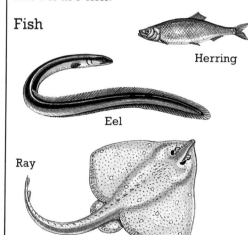

Herring
Eel
Ray

Fish are cold-blooded, which means that their bodies stay the same temperature as their surroundings. They vary a lot in shape, but they nearly all have fins and live in water, breathing through gills. Some live in fresh water; others in the sea.

Amphibians

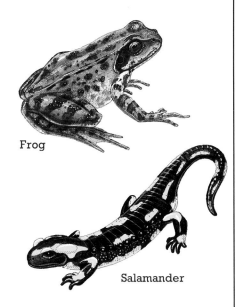

Frog

Salamander

Amphibians are cold-blooded and have smooth, moist skins without scales or feathers. They can live on land as well as in water, but they have to return to the water to breed. Frogs, toads, salamanders and newts are all amphibians.

Reptiles

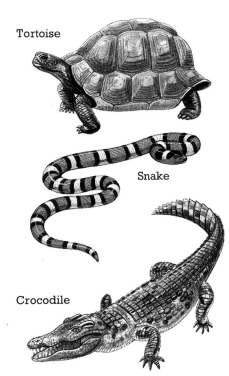

Tortoise

Snake

Crocodile

Reptiles are cold-blooded and have scaly skins. They live on land as well as in water, but unlike amphibians they lay eggs. Snakes, lizards, tortoises, turtles and crocodiles are reptiles. Many are carnivorous and eat other animals.

Birds

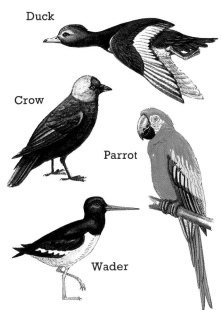

Duck

Crow

Parrot

Wader

Birds are warm-blooded, which means that their bodies stay the same temperature, regardless of their surroundings. Birds are the only animals with feathers (but their legs are scaly). All of them have wings and most of them can fly.

Mammals

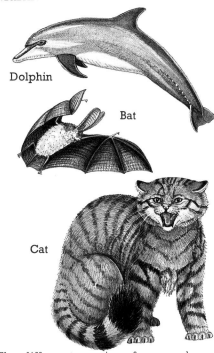

Dolphin

Bat

Cat

The different species of mammals vary enormously, ranging from the dolphin to the bat, and the elephant to the dog. They are warm-blooded and the only animals with hair or fur. They feed their newborn babies on milk and have well-developed senses and brains. Rodents, marsupials and primates are different groups of mammals.

Rodents

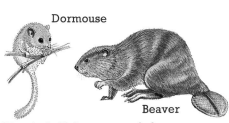

Dormouse

Beaver

Nearly half the mammals known are rodents. Rodent means "gnawing teeth" and all rodents have sharp front teeth. Mice, beavers, chipmunks and squirrels are rodents. Some of them eat plants and others are scavengers.

Marsupials

Koala

Kangaroo

Kangaroos, wombats and koala bears are all marsupials. Female marsupials have a "pouch" on their undersides. When their babies are born, they are still not fully formed and they finish growing inside their mother's warm pouch.

Primates

Bush baby

Orangutan

Chimpanzee

Lemurs, bush babies, monkeys, apes and humans are all primates. Most of them are tree-dwellers and live in tropical rain forests. They look alike, have grasping hands and good eyesight and are more intelligent than most of the other types of mammals.

INDEX